Status Update

Status Update

by

Sarah Yi-Mei Tsiang

OOLICHAN BOOKS
FERNIE, BRITISH COLUMBIA, CANADA
2013

Library and Archives Canada Cataloguing in Publication

Tsiang, Sarah, 1978-, author

    Status update / Sarah Yi-Mei Tsiang.

Poems.

ISBN 978-0-88982-296-2 (pbk.)

    I. Title.

PS8639.S583S83 2013   C811'.6   C2013-905851-6

We gratefully acknowledge the financial support of the Canada Council for
the Arts, the British Columbia Arts Council through the BC Ministry of
Tourism, Culture, and the Arts, and the Government of Canada through
the Book Publishing Industry Development Program, for our publishing
activities.

Published by
Oolichan Books
P.O. Box 2278
Fernie, British Columbia
Canada V0B 1M0

www.oolichan.com

Cover design by Michael Hepher of Clawhammer Press, Fernie, B.C.
www.clawhammer.com.

Printed in Canada.

The poems contained herein are inspired by Facebook posts by actual
persons. The poems themselves bear no relationship to actual people
and any resemblance to actual persons, living or dead, or actual events is
purely coincidental.

For Tim: these poems and my love

Ungemmed, unhidden, wishing not to hurt,
As one should bring you cowslips in a hat
Swung from the hand, or apples in her skirt,
I bring you, calling out as children do:
"Look what I have!—And these are all for you."

Edna St. Vincent Millay (Sonnet XI)

Table of Contents

Emily Polh-Weary thinks everything seems insignificant once she's posted it on Facebook.

Like · Comment · Share · 33 minutes ago

Julie Bruck At SF Friends School, the 7th graders get an ethical question every week. This week's was "Is it wrong to lie to a dog?" Due Friday.

Like · Comment · Share · about an hour ago

The dog knows when you lie.
All your plans, every time
you go for a walk alone.

He can smell it on you,
the wind in your jacket,
the hotdog on your breath.

Still, his love is like a loose leash.
There is no moment when he is not tethered
to you. His paws go slack
over your feet as you lie
in bed, listening

to your mind recite reasons you're alone.
He pretends, for you, that you are both
happy, that the ten minute walks
around the same city block
can fill your hearts.

Susan Musgrave has an unrequited urge to be lonely.

Like · Comment · Share · 2 minutes ago

Remember that part of you, alone,
the sound of your breath
against a ragged scarf
of wind.

Even in your sleep they track you,
twinned breaths, your granddaughters
and their pulsing fontanelles.

Turn in bed, the furnace hums
a slow song, thinks about the
nature of fire. The babies' fingers
unfurl, trace the shape of your
heat in their sleep.

Your daughter, heavy with milk,
dreams about a circle in sand,
coyotes. Their voices are an ache,
a keening hunger. She will sing the babies
to the closed cradle of her heart,
lull the tricksters, fill their bellies
with the moon.

Remember what it is to walk
along the crest of a cold ocean,
pebbles underfoot, water that reaches
for you, before it pulls back,
finds itself.

Julie H oh sweet hayzeus, tuesday huh? this week is going to drag like heartache...

Like · Comment · Share · 3 hours ago

We peer over cubicle walls high as snow drifts.
Computer fans shush like a desperate mother,
trying to lull her own violence
into rest.

The coffee maker sits and watches
the strangled line of mourners visit its small altar.
It is the only philosopher
in the building. Repeats its mantra:
the action of emptiness.

Tuesday, say the calendars,
crossing themselves.
There is no candle to light,
no faith to rattle our small coins.

Paul Vermeersch "After one has abandoned a belief in God, poetry is that essence which takes its place as life's redemption." — Wallace Stevens

Like · Comment · Share · about an hour ago

You, a mouthful of bells,

a call to prayer that rings out
to the righteous, silences
the mongrel dogs.

I want you to name the stars
for me, to conjure loaves and fish
for the multitudes of my hunger.

But you contend that hunger
and faith are two different animals:
one a song-bird,
            hollow-boned
the other a scavenger,
            thick and sated.

You don't say which is which.

I am tired of your
hollow box of confession,
prayers, small words of smoke
caught in the rafters.

            Open my chest, find the heart
            and its crown of thorns. Find the light
            that fires it.

Watch the baptized file past,
throats exposed and pink like hatchlings.

See them hold the word close,
dissolving on their tongues.
Open their mouths and find nothing
but breath, sweet yeast.

> Open my chest, find the heart
> in its nest of blood. Find the air
> that arrests it.

Duke Lang ...yes, the cocoon of it, your "body outgrowing its own sorrow"[1]...

Like · Comment · Share · 5 hours ago

Look through the sympathy cards:
pastels, oceans and clouds.
Eloquent peace, God.
Appeals to your sense
of faith.

What a poverty of words.
If I were honest, I'd tell you
that you will never get over
this grief.

You are damaged.
His death is a wide wound
that will fester. Healing means new skin,
scars, an ache in the body
when it rains, or snows, or when age sets in;
and we know more by our loss
than our remaining senses.

Every time we access a memory,
we change it.
The people we have lost
become distant echoes
of our own voices
every time we try to name them.

---

[1]This unattributed quotation is taken from a Susan Musgrave poem, "One-Sided Woman", which can be found on page 92 of her Collected Poems, _What The Small Day Cannot Hold_.

We make poor copies
of those we loved.

What's left to us are those copies,
hundreds of tattered revisions,
torn pages, over and over again,
his face, his face, his face.

Julie Bruck Driving home on a wet Friday
afternoon. Girl in front seat, yacking. Paper bag of
bagels in back, and enough new ink cartridges to
last well into 2010. Wealth.

Like · Comment · Share · about an hour ago

November, look at all you let go:

The days release
their loose grip, the trees abandon
leaves on our doorsteps.
Milkweed opens like a coinpurse
and spends all it has.
The unfettered air and its arms
of wind can hold on
to nothing.

But still, November lingers, gives us this:

> the drive home on a wet Friday afternoon,
> gloss of her damp hair, tumble
> of words, the bag of fresh bagels,
> patient tick of the heaters.

November teaches us to hold.

Adrienne Gruber does not understand why the congested dreams she has have to be filled with murder. Why murder, why? (2)

Like · Comment · Share · 2 minutes ago via BlackBerry

The bright congestion of sunlight on a noon street,
a man being beat to death with a baseball bat
to the tune of a radio, in the distance.

In my dreams I am the spectator,
behind curtains, my clumsy fingers thick as hammers
on the shifting numbers of the dial pad

and I am the man on the street,
muscles tight with the sweet spot
of the bat, the thick resistance of the body

and I am the man on the street,
holding together the unravelling seams
of my skull with one hand,

reaching for the bat with the other.
It goes on for hours, the night clocked by
this endless murder and even within

it, I know it's a dream. But as I wake
it's the radio I can't shake off,
a distant

hollow pop tune,
singing to no one
but itself.

Emily Pohl-Weary "I'm an old fashioned gal. I was raised to believe that men dig up the corpses and women have the babies." — Buffy

Like · Comment · Share · July 19 at 11:47pm

Skeleton park sonnet[2]

Men dig up the corpses, white as raw
potatoes. Grave robbers have left
a pebbled trail of emptied teeth. Consider the heft
of a forearm, the foot fit in by saw

bodies softened like meat after a thaw.
The workers are going home dazed, bereft;
their wives are a graveyard, skin cleft
into narrow trenches, their hands frail claws.

Put up swings over the bodies, fix slides
into the graveyard's soft mouth. Who better
to catch the children? Ghosts have so little

to do these days. Mothers and their asides,
their cooled coffees, their silent love letters
to bones, children, their lives breaking brittle.

---

[2]This sonnet is based on Skeleton park in Kingston, Ontario. The park is
built over an overcrowded cemetery. Workers tried to remove and rebury
the bodies but eventually gave up on the project. On occasion human
remains will be found on the grass.

Julie Bruck P.K. Page has died at 93. I think they broke the mold.

Like · Comment · Share · Yesterday at 9:51pm

The whole world is a cup
one could hold in one's hand like a stone
warmed by that same summer sun
but the dead or the near dead
                    P.K. Page's "Autumn"

Small movements, heartbeats
of an unconscious life.
What brings me down the stairs
and measures coffee? What moves my hand
to find the newspaper, crisp and folded,
a tidy rubber band round it? Sunup,
open the eyes of the heart, count
what's left. Love, you are gone,
and the whole world contracts to this knife, this egg, this ketchup.
The whole world is a cup.

I am contained in this body;
all of us move in the spheres of our grief,
our private joys. Look at the mailman and his dizzying
happiness, the housewife next door, her heart a trembling needle
on a string, swinging between joy and terror. The child on the sidewalk
draws herself in chalk, and it crumbles as easily as my bones.
I am contained by this grief until the day I think
of overdue books, the price of pears, a moment without you,
and this betrayal cleaves me. You, a heaviness, alone
one could hold in one's hand like a stone.

Time skulks around the house
like a cat, pouncing on the shadows.
I will not let it out for the night, not
open my door in the morning to find
evidence of its wandering, unseen stars
caught and dying on his coat. I will not run
after him, calling. Let time hunt
his mice. I am unraveling my life,
a thread of knots that fall undone
warmed by that same summer sun

which burned long before
we had eyes to see it. My love,
I could count a thousand times this hour —
I have turned to your absence,
as bright and unmoving as the sun. I used to be able
to mouth your words before they were said,
and now, days and weeks and years after your death,
I rattle your words, last grains of rice in a tin,
left to beg of my memory. What is left to be fed
but the dead, or the near dead?

Jennifer Coon has returned from an epic journey.

Like · Comment · Share · about an hour ago

Windchimes on a bare tree;
returning home and leaving it.

Who knew there could be such sweet notes
in our hollowed bodies?

Bonita Summers Astrology - Today's Cancer
Horoscope: You've been mulling something over lately.

You're waiting for her.
It's nearly 5 in the morning.
The sun is loosening
night's hard-tucked edges.

That time when the stars run
out of breath.
It is such a long way

to travel. A beacon after
everything is gone. Star gazing is nothing
but standing at a wake,
listening to light's elegy.

Your eldest daughter, getting out
of a car that rolls away too quickly.
Shadow stains the creases of her eyes.
You walk into the house,
make tea. You are both
so tired.

You watch her drink, carefully,
her worn mouth
working around its silences.

She is still the sum
of your heart. And you,
you are nothing but
a poor astrologist,
reading the constellations
of her face, over and over
trying to find yourself
in that lost light.

Emily Pohl-Weary Breathe.

Here is the poet:
there is nothing to do but listen
to your own breath
the easy way you let go
of what keeps you alive.

Your breath, the air of everyone
in this room, like communion,
placed in the open mouths
of strangers, a shared
body of air.

Think of how many breaths
have left you, have gone
out into the world bearing
the shape of your lungs,
the squeeze of your cells.

Your breaths line the corridors
of office buildings, the uplift
of the swings in City park.
Your breaths sit in hospital waiting rooms,
bated, used over and over again
and held close, a rosary
for the new widow's lungs.

Listen to your breath.

This is what the poet was trying to say.

Alice Burdick Hazel, to a toy fish in a colander:
"Don't talk; you're not real."

Like · Comment · Share · 11 minutes ago

The toy fish mutters to itself in the colander,
"I am drowned"
and sometimes "Hello?"
and sometimes he is as solemn as a Magic 8 Ball
predicting that the outlook is not good.

The family pretends they can't hear it.
They talk louder and with more enthusiasm
over dinner, where their forks and plates
stay mercifully silent.

In the evenings, the fish keeps everyone awake,
thrashing in the toy box, gasping for air.
It quotes Rumi to calm itself. It is an educated fish;
and always more philosophical in the evening.
The dolls lean, tip their eyes shut,
but there is no closing the sound

of its insistent voice:
Now sleeping, now awake,
my heart is in constant fervor.
It is a covered saucepan, placed on fire.

The fish is left in the bathtub,
while the family pretends it is still just a toy,
ignores the hollow thumping
of its body against the ceramic,

that damned fish, swimming
through their dreams,
wearing the water thin.

Leanne Leiberman Well, it rained in my kitchen today,

Like · Comment · Share · November 19 at 9:36 pm

A sudden sprinkling, the ceiling
bulges like pregnant clouds.

This will cost thousands.
And my slippers are drowning.

The children clamour for toast,
and the ruined butter undoes me.

Not even this, not even *this*
survives the morning.

How could we not notice
how bared we are to the sky?

The pots gather water, fill
themselves. Open mouths

to the ceiling, like children
tasting snow. The two boys

in our sodden kitchen
float boats in the frying pan.

They are delighted with the open
sky, the tipping ark

of plastic animals. The youngest
dons his water wings,

a dove, gliding over
the end of the world.

Abby Shantz looking at the yearbook.... we've changed ALOT since grade 7 XD

Like · Comment · Share · Yesterday at 1:56pm

All those songs we knew by heart,
recess and the endless rope
of grade school. Remember
how we could lose ourselves
in play? Our minds'
constellations of the possible.

In the mirror, after a bath,
map a new geography:
the body swell, a tidal force.
There are continents within.

Childhood is a country left behind.
The old fables, superstitions, the law
of faith. The untamed thickets of our hearts.

Distance proves nothing. Passports,

clothes, a new language.
The only thing that remains
are the stars, silent witnesses
to our lost songs

Timmy Toe Tag Sometimes it just feels soooooo good to tell the right person to "go F*CK themselves!" Try it out sometime!!

Like · Comment · Share · 2 hours ago near Toronto, Ontario

After a while, he can't help himself. He whispers *fuck you* to the toast, that beige fucker that just lies there, passive aggressive in its thin housecoat of yellow margarine. *Fuck you* to the cloud puffs that imitate children's scrawled drawings, those lazy clichés in the crayola-blue sky. *Fuck you* to the elevator, whose "close door" button is worn with animosity. *Fuck you* to the nagging dent in the car door, to the grass that shrivels and wilts under August's unrelenting parental glare. *Fuck you* to the Internet's kittys and porn. *Fuck you* to the washing machine's solo hula dance, to the turtle's blunt and beautiful head. *Fuck you*, and the dog sings it with him, longing at the gate. And the seagulls toss it back and forth, red throats gleaming. *Fuck you* until it becomes as soft as a mantra, until is loosens into a hundred small prayers every day. *Fuck you*, and it is as tender as a newborn's head, as the act of love, as our first beginning.

Andrew Pyper Justin Bieber grew up in my home town of Stratford, where a "paternity suit" was just a girl shouting "Asshole!" at some guy at Smokers Corner.

Like · Comment · Share · 43 minutes ago

You would like it to be more like the movies,
where the couple reclines against the hood of the car
between the gleaming city and the stars,
in the middle of the sky.

Instead, you never leave the car,
and there is a *thunk* as the seat reclines.
There are mosquitoes, one caught in the brambles
of your hair, as he fumbles the catch
on your bra.

Still, it is enough: his skin baby-soft,
the sparse hair above his lip
a translucent blond, glimmering
in the low lights of the parking lot.

His weight on you, the car's upholstery
weaving its pattern on the back of your neck.
At home you will examine all he has left,
the slight blue of a hickey,
a wisp of Irish Spring on your skin,
the inexorable changes

of your body, after.

Search the window: you are still
young enough to wish on stars. A solitary

light punching through dusky clouds,
winking like a beacon.

Pin your hopes to the sky,
your star moving away from you,
nothing but a dimming light
on the wing.

Sue Fisher Muriel has infinity babies in her
tummy and they are being born NOW!

Like · Comment · Share · December 4, 2009 at 11:08am

Tumble of babies,
sweet-cheeked, open-eyed.

My daughter and her expansive
womb, the endless possibilities

of birth. What stories we tell—
immaculate deliveries, haze

of blurred photos. The sloppy-
after-grin, clean hospital blankets.

But love, my darling, love does not come
easily. Love is what is borne

in those small hours, counting
the rise and fall of your breath,

counting the ounces you lost,
the toe-curling pain of your latch.

Love is what is born
when we can no longer bear

and yet we do.

Dave Hickey A good night to pretend you're a
lighthouse keeper.

Like · Comment · Share · 5 minutes ago

There are nights when the fog
creeps over the couches,
soaks the living room
in pregnant clouds.

How to navigate the house?
Children slumber like rocks,
immovable and exposed.

You are always at the edge
of something. Light the lamps
and watch for ships.

You cannot see beyond
the windows, beyond your
children held up and displayed
by your bright lamps,
your small glass enclosure.

Outside, ships falter
in the haze of water and air.
Tomorrow, children will scavenge the shore
for our bones and shipwrecks.

Emily Pohl-Weary What should we do with all
the memories?

Like · Comment · Share · Yesterday at 11:23pm

Tie them to strings, a short
tether between you and the sky.
Let them tug and change
the course of clouds
like a hand skimming still water.

Let them crowd the house,
jostle against the closed ceiling
of your life.

And keep your fist tight
around the bundle, even
if thin wires bite
into the soft underbelly
of your hand.

You'll never hold on to them all.
You won't even notice
what leaves you,
blends into the blue
of an empty sky.

But mourn every time
your grip loosens.

Mandy Reid Back to work for the night

Palliative care, where we teach
patients to swim.
Our voices are the confident muscle
of bathing-capped instructors:
turn over now Mr. Mason,
just a little further Mrs. Getty.

As they see our blurred
white feet, hear the whistle
garbled from another
dimension.

The business of dying happens mainly at night.
It's the body adapting to another element,
the shock of cold becomes a numbness,
a new body until
you surface, and the air snatches you back.

Morphine deepens the water,
moves all the markers you counted,
makes you forget when to turn
your head, where to take
a breath.

Pain management: we show you how
there can be distances
between yourself and yourself
how easy it is to let go
of what once defined you.

Ada Mullett is standing at a podium waiting 2 more minutes before starting her stats class

Like · Comment · Share · 59 minutes ago

Welcome.

Let's talk about statistics. Statistics are more than just numbers. In the social sciences they allow us to see what's going on in the world. Say, 1 in 4 women will be sexually assaulted in their lifetimes. But what does that mean? Does that mean that someone in this class will definitely be sexually assaulted? No. It all has to do with probabilities.

For instance, what if the woman is disabled? Then she has a 83%[3] probability of being sexually assaulted in her lifetime.

What if the woman comes from a lower socioeconomic background? What if she is native? Then we're talking a 24?%[4] probability within these past five years. What if the woman, as a girl, witnessed her mother, broken-winged, on the tiles, trying to mop up her own blood? What if she's spent time in a shelter? What if she's been on the street because the shelter is full and she followed this guy to a new town and there are no couches she could sleep on? What if she has a baby, who cries, a dark wet mouth of hunger? What if she is afraid?

What if the woman, her body howling for another fix, her feet numb on the sidewalk, sees the car slow down? What if she charges twenty instead of ten? What if she looks inside, sees the carseat drowning in crumbs, the carcasses of juice

[3]http://sacha.ca/fact-sheets/statistics
[4]http://publications.gc.ca/collections/Collection-R/Statcan/85-002-XIE/85-002-XIE2006003.pdf

boxes? She'll likely be in the 68%[5] percent of sex workers who are raped on the job.

What if she's in University? We know that 80% of female undergraduates, most of you, have been victims of violence.[6] But what if he is sweet? What if he walks her to her dorm room, and he kisses her, lightly at first. What if she changes her mind? What if she is drunk? What if he had a bad day? What if his buddies told him he had a small dick and then laughed? What if the hall light sputters and her roommate is gone and that drink, the peach schnapps mix he handed her, makes her legs feel numb? What if she doesn't remember and so she doesn't fall into the 29%[7] who actually report their incidents of sexual assault?

What if she lives in Vancouver's eastside? What if she never left Owen Sound? What if her mom told her that sometimes guys can't stop? What if her father loved her?

---

[5] http://sacha.ca/fact-sheets/statistics
[6] http://sacha.ca/fact-sheets/statistics
[7] http://sacha.ca/fact-sheets/statistics

Susan Musgrave is humbled by the fact that one teaspoon of honey represents the life's work of twelve bees.

Like · Comment · Share · 10 hours ago

1
First flight, a dropped sky
of boundless air,
freedom in duty.

2
Such silence, after
the hive. Startling,
the noise within us.

3
Constellations of clover
in a sky
of grass

4
Fallen apples,
the stumble-sweet
of autumn.

5
Hold more than you can
carry. Give over
sweetness, again.

6
Winter huddle, we are
one body, a thin
shiver.

7
Spring. The heavy
head of flowers,
waking lovers.

8
Air, sky, shimmer
of moon. How
to be alone.

9
The long throat
of honeysuckle;
love makes you crawl.

10
Summer evening,
the wing flutter
of stars.

11
First frost
and even the flowers
are stunned.

12
Death comes like rain;
a sudden heaviness
of wings.

Dave Hickey Great day for ducks!

Like · Comment · Share · October 2, 2009 at 11:32am

A yellow slip of a day,
sunlight cocked at a jaunty angle,
the ducks mooning
us as we walk.

Headstands underwater, and
all summer my daughter
has demanded my feet in the air,
the waddled walk of hands
over thick mud, seaweed.

Now wind whips the first
leaves off the trees, a burlesque
of maples throwing us their
caterpillar-laced underwear.

How fine we are!
Tossing our youth into the air,
watching it fall,
like brittle leaves,
all around us.

Jennifer Coon Happy Steal Something From Work Day!

Like · Comment · Share · 4 hours ago

There is nothing you own here.
Even the earth's slow progression
around the sun is leased.

The woman beside you hammers
her keyboard like an angry lover,
each letter a reproach, a grudging
giving-over.

What do you know about her?
The smell of her hair: dandruff shampoo
and hair spray, the clump of mascara that edges
her eyes. The rhythm of her
breath. The whisking sound
of her pantyhose as she shifts.
Her sigh, loose and unwinding.

Details, horrible and intimate.
You spend your days trying to replace
everything you have stolen
from her — like a married couple,
courteous, making room for each other
in the hall.

We are left with nothing
after the fire.
The insurance man asks us
to name our losses.

My memory places its blind fingers
on what was in our bedroom,
the list a scribbled searchlight
that pans across burnt and broken rooms.

The hollowed closets, wire skeletons
with imagined clothes. Neat boxes of ornaments,
photographs, cards I couldn't throw out.

In the very back,
the blue plastic tub I refused
to look at: the tiny yellow sleepers,
a rubber giraffe still in its box.

I catalogue:
The first one, the flutter,
life as small as a thumb,
her heart and mine, quickening.

But I know the rules;
you can't claim something you never had.

Sue Fisher I burned it.

Like · Comment · Share · Yesterday at 8:30pm

I burned bras, a bonfire of lace sparking in elegant whorls, fireworks of speech until all that was left were the clasps and underwire, a metal skeleton of breasts, a cage whose smoke whimpered words like *lift* and *support* and *push up* as though tits were children who need help up the slide and I burned books, the gleeful and sadistic voices of parenting experts curling and blackening like when I burned dinner watching my girl push away my nipple, head the colour of an egg, the colour of milk, the colour of the emptiness that was drying up inside my ducts, and I burned midnight oil with her, both of us smoking dreams, high with our eyes half open, the half life of scorched nights, her cries a scatter bomb, stuffed animals dispersed like casualties over a hand-knit rug, and I burned bridges, tossing a torch over my shoulder every time we crossed anything, her childhood always the far side of a river, my memory a crumbling bridge of ashes, and I burned witches in her closet, her fever glimmering like coals in my chest, I ripped apart the room as if I could find the monsters we both saw there, and I burned

Barbara-Anne Pender Robertson On our way
to urgent care with a sick little boy :(

Like · Comment · Share · Yesterday at 4:22pm

He is in the car seat, buckled
into safety,
immobile in a snowsuit
that makes his arms and legs
stick out at angles; a starfish.
His breath bubbles
at the surface of his lips.

We are driving through
snow and stop lights.
The moon peeks one eye through
fingers of dark clouds.

And in this car, this small room
made of glass and metal
we are buckled together,
counting his broken breaths.

Let this ride be over,
let this ride take all the hours
left in my heart.

Susan Musgrave I don't know how much lonelier it gets than this. We can never know how much another person is suffering. There was a memorial service for Tanya, yesterday, in Victoria. She sent her last manuscript of poems to Richard Olafson the day before, saying, "Do what you like with these."

Like · Comment · Share · Sat at 12:51pm

Imagine the mother. She searches for a daughter
made to marry, forced down the long orchard to the well. No child
in a white dress. Her mouth goes blind, stitches the web of evening
in distress. She doesn't see the new tree, one arm outstretched.

Tanya Kern's "Other"

This is the one place you are not
lost. Trees bending while night shadows
drip over your shoulders. Dusk, a jackknife opening.
The gloss of light parts from
between the trees. Like the hollow glen
in your chest. Everything is filled with water
flowing away from its source. When did that spring
dry up? What were the names that hung by your door?
There are none now. Each has been slaughtered.
Imagine the mother. She searches for a daughter

in the forest of her heart. Where are her children?
Everything is overgrown, brambles and chokecherry,
the dark rustling of hunger.
Cut away the undergrowth. Stop your search.
There is no one here, even you are not
here. Your knife is blunt against the wild

lushness that blots out the light. There are no breadcrumbs
back to your house, no father who led you here.
The path you cut is your own. No one beguiled,
made to marry, forced down the long orchard to the well. No child

at your skirts. There is no one. What were the names you turned out
before you locked the door? Let them fend for themselves.
You cannot make your way back. Your hands are torn,
too many children, a hard man. Sit a little longer and listen
to the stars, huddled in their own warm homes, light years
away from you. You remember, faintly, the songs they sing,
the smell of your daughter's hair, still wet
from the bath. The taste of her blood
on a skinned knee. One woman's life bound in sap rings,
in a white dress. Her mouth goes blind, stitches the web of evening

closer until there is nothing to see, stars recede
behind clouds. You, she, her
names fall from that mute mouth. They never belonged
in this forest. There was never anything
but the distant wolves, a moon that shrinks
from itself. All scars were already etched
in the trees, they simply grew around their wounds.
Lie down at the base of the pine. Strip your sleeves,
your wrists are bark. Leave those names here, take the knife and etch
in distress. She doesn't see the new tree, one arm outstretched.

Dave Genge It's amazing how kids relate to things. Anna looked out at the fog this morning and said, "wow, our campfire sure is smoky."

Like · Comment · Share · September 29 at 7:49am

The lake smoulders,
a deep, burnt blue.

Leaves crackle like fire,
as maples pull the alarm.

The sun is the only thing
left whole,

rising with the loons,
placid as a stone.

It is the hand-over hour,
night's gleaming

face scrubbed clean
and leaving.

Anna struggles out of her sleeping
bag, clears the smoke

of night from her eyes. This morning,
she sees the whole world

as it is: on fire,
crumbling to ashes.

John Lofranco Woah.

www.telegraph.co.uk

A 13-year-old Croatian girl who fell into a coma
woke up speaking fluent German.

Like · Comment · Share · about an hour ago

What languages lie unbidden
within us? Imagine what it is
to wake within another
language, like finding someone
else's glasses on your bedside table.

Within you, all the languages
of the dead. All the words
of the stars. When you reach
out in the dark room

your heart speaks in tongues.
When you open your mouth
what comes is another word,
so close to the one you meant,

but from another country.
Love, you say, and it is a marvel
that someone can flip through the dictionary
and come up with a translation,
a word that used to sound familiar.

Michael Leary A parsec is a unit of distance, not time. Stupid Han Solo.

Like · Comment · Share · about an hour ago

How to measure the lengths
between us?

This is a small house
of great distances.

Look at our bedroom;
you are calling from a far country,

a voice full of static
as the operator demands

another thousand coins.

Noelle Allen needs to read a whole lot of manuscripts, and unfortunately, write some rejection letters.

Like · Comment · Share · 15 minutes ago

Dear Sarah,

While we read your manuscript with interest, it doesn't fit with our publishing mandate. Maybe if it had more tomatoes, ripening on the vine. Or if the protagonist had paused on page 36 and let the sky burnish her face into something as smooth and relatable as the moon.

Perhaps if your father had died a year earlier, or a year later, you would have written those passages with your heart clenched tight as a fist. You would have fully captured that hollow echo in your chest that still wakes you at night, ringing long and loose, your heart a clapper that can't forget the metallic moment of contact.

That can't forget, but all you wrote was the echo, not the moment the bell tolled.

We needed the bell to toll.

There were parts of your writing that we found interesting. We enjoyed reading the poem about that time you fell into the bonfire, your father reaching into the flames, calmly. How when you came out, parts of his palm had melted into your own skin. When we meet you at a party years later we will try our best not to stare at the delicate, whorled scars burned into your upper arm. We will try not to remember you, or your book, as a wild scatter of ashes and flesh.

If you write another book, about something else, please consider sending it to us.

Sincerely,
The Editors

Sarah Pelton has been unfriended...interesting...

I've been lost before,
and worse. Remember the corn maze?

Somehow separated from you
I hatched wild plans to live on cow corn,

create a husk of a house. Later you asked
why I didn't simply cut through,

and once again I'm lost
for an answer.

Somehow you know all the things
I don't. I want to tell you

that I called and called,
convinced you were as lost as me.

I want to tell you how I could have
cried with relief, seeing the end

of it, the sudden sky, a house in the distance.
But you were already in the car, flipping

through a magazine. Behind me the maze,
my imagined life without you.

Emily Pohl-Weary What's the most treacherous terrain?

Like · Comment · Share · Sat at 9:43am

> **Kerry Lambie** Dating!
>
> Like · Comment · Share · Sat at 3:08pm
>
> **Vincent Tinguely** Loose shale on a steep slope, yo.
>
> Like · Comment · Share · Sat at 5:56pm
>
> **Ann Pohl** Motherhood: the newborn human who is crying and you don't have a friggin' clue what "that" cry means. Also apparently the snowmobile trails in BC.
>
> Like · Comment · Share · Yesterday at 1:04pm

That cry is a cliff's edge,
the slip-sound of shale
loosening underfoot.

Remember stars over the hood
of his car? The drop-off below,
the way your heart could plummet
and catch itself when his hand
slipped over your thigh?

You thought then that your heart
had no bounds. The sky and the endless
autumn air. The plunge over, and over.

But there are so many ways of falling.
Here, in this kitchen, the floor
rolling away from you. Who knows
why the baby cries,

or what those cries have triggered
in you, your chest a slow tumbling,
an avalanche over her crib,
obliterating both of you.

Sue Goyette We are always setting out, as if to discover where the map ends will allow us to begin. hornbook G -Kroetsch

For what is likely our last trip, I pack like a fortune teller,
and throw in enough to cover all the star's possibilities.
Of course, you don't need Tums, extra shoes, or tiny sewing kits.
You know that a handful of thread won't keep us
from unravelling. You point to a hole
in your sweater; you've worn it bare.
It takes practise to expose oneself to the world. But, oh, I can imagine
all your disasters: tattered, sun-burned, your heart
stuttering and thick without daily blood thinners. I pack it all with care
into the extra shoes we will never wear.

On the highway all tragedy is laid out.
Ribbons and plastic flowers tied around road signs,
a teddy bear and poem affixed to a weathered white cross.
You stop the car, stand bent in the rain, read
that earnest poem wrapped in yellowing plastic. You still don't believe
every goodbye is the same. We are all on that cliff's
edge. Passing trucks shake the car senseless, and you wrestle off
your jacket before getting back in. The wind blows its own
      shape in your clothes.
Your mother, you tell me, used to open her coat and try to
      catch the wind like a skiff.
We are always setting out, as if

the road could unwind itself into something else,
or your mother could have caught the wind,
wrapped tight and struggling, boxing for freedom.
You are dying, and the highway goes on without us.

I've put all my faith in restless maps, the futile
folding of pages that never snap back. I would like to send
ourselves into a mapped land. A definitive
you are here. But our markers move,
landmarks crumble. We only pretend
to discover where the maps end,

when all we have is the tiny, to-scale ratio of how far
we've travelled to be here. Still, you are teaching me to love driving
without a map. To get lost. To love the countless
fields with sleepy-eyed cows, the weeds all tangled up
in the prairie's last light. The city roads slick with rain,
streetlights imitating the stars, winking to no one. Alleys so thin
we can see their cobbled bones as we pass. Your careless hand
    surfing the air's current.
Every turn is a lesson on the infinite roads to nowhere. *This*, you say,
your mother's coat, the lost street, the wind skimming your skin;
will allow us to begin.

Hollay Ghadery Left our grocery list in the cart. Not out of laziness, but because I love finding other people's lists. Hope someone appreciates the quite serious "Sleeping cot for man 300lbs+" item.

Like · Comment · Share · March 19 at 7:53pm

In the cart, a list of someone else's life.
Scrawled letters, an upturn at the base
of every word. This is a man
who writes alone, who buys milk
in a small carton. His cats
eat premium cat food.

This is a man without a beard,
a man who will set his environmentally-
conscious bags on the counter,
and open his skinny cow ice cream treat
before he puts away his groceries.

This is a man who knows all the stars
by name, who watches the soothing optimism
of the slap-chop salesman at 3am. A man who takes
Nytol with sleepy time tea and dreams
a void, nights filled with easy blanks.

This is a man who shops on Thursdays,
who has plans for tomorrow, who wants
to make spaghetti from scratch. His tomatoes
are organic. There is a woman, maybe,
or another man, who will eat this spaghetti,

who will sop up the sauce with a crust
of garlic bread. Who will lean over
the table, singeing their shirt on the single candle,
and taste his mouth:
flesh, full and sweet.

Susan Musgrave "A casual stroll through lunatic asylums shows that faith does not prove anything." — Nietzsche

Like · Comment · Share · Yesterday at 12:31pm

Look what lived inside me:
a tight heartbeat, a screaming
that wakes the neighbours.
Oh red-faced banshee,
I let you out.

Walk with me.
It is thirty-two steps
to the end
of the living room, and
seventeen to the kitchen.
A rosary of tiles;
absolution is beyond
her voice.

Walk the room until
there is a groove in the floor.
Until the hum in my throat
can float on without me. Faith,
faith, that nothing is infinite.

Jessica Michalofsky Why does oatmeal?
Wherefore coffee? How branches in sunlight
morning pink? How lipidly red and flippant are
leaves in morning wind? How calmcool blue
november sky day.

Like · Comment · Share · 8 minutes ago

Now, the oatmeal, the branches
caught in sunlight. A million questions
the morning poses, and the unanswerable day.

My husband and daughter sleep
and their morning dreams gather
a backdrop of blue November sky,
cool as a foot stuck out of the covers.

My daughter will wake first,
half-formed words tossed off;
the language of birds. She always wakes within
a dream, frantic to translate
the night's efforts.

My husband will be next,
blind feelers searching the space
I've left. Morning defined by absence.
He wakes not knowing who he is,
but able to name all that is missing.

Annie MacKenzie sent you a Pet Society request: I need help with the Squirrel Tree Home. Please can you send me a Roof, I won't forget it!

Like · Comment · Share · 15 minutes ago

At work, you are suddenly aware of your mouse.
It is an egg: smooth and precise. It fits your palm
and radiates a sleepy body-warmth.
There is a blood clot shining through
the hard shell. Evidence of life.

On the walk home the night sky is a thin mud.
Light puddles from the streetlamps.
You would like to roll in it. Feel the foggy
softness of the evening.

In your condo, your cat lolls in comfortable complicity.
There are no mice, and you each avoid the subject
of your own dubious purpose.

Take the dog for a walk. Even he is reduced,
leg bent, pointing to yield signs. Convinced
he can startle them into flight.

Darryl Joel (DJ) Berger, artist and writer Do
we shudder at getting older or do we grieve for
our youth?

Like · Comment · Share · 10 minutes ago

In the backyard snowfort
my daughter has gathered her supplies:
a bucket, skipping ropes, empty soda cans.
This is all she needs to survive.

Her mittens carve out the ceiling.
It's in my bones too — a slow hollowing,
an ache as the snow shifts and settles.

I once spent hours, a lifetime
of hot woollen breaths,
sweeping loose snow
from a house that begins a slow
arch above me.

Children are like this;
sculpting themselves from snow
while we wait at the window,
hoping it won't collapse.

Ashley-Elizabeth Best Days are just drops in the river to be lost always. Only you, only you, you know

Like · Comment · Share · 13 hours ago

Late October and the river is white-capped,
swept by the wind like dirt under a broom.

Still, the geese are faithful. They stand by the river
in a stubborn marriage, unwilling to admit the fall.

Last year the river froze so suddenly
that some birds were trapped, half buried

in ice. There should be a lesson in this, but even now
the forecast calling for a cold snap, and

the geese and I are heedless,
standing vigil to the loss of days.

Deb Franke "Suddenly I realize / That if I stepped out of my body I would break / Into blossom." — James Wright.

Like · Comment · Share · Yesterday at 7:47pm

That is delicate as the skin over a girl's wrist
Suddenly I realize
That if I stepped out of my body I would break
Into blossom
                        James Wright's "Blessing"

All day she has been at me,
trudging around the house,
my arms filled with laundry as she nudges
my legs like a colt trying to get under her mother.
There is never an arms-length of peace.
She is all elbows and knees, her fists
open and close, trying to grasp
the wisps of attention I toss her.
How many ways have I broken her? All I've dismissed,
that is delicate as the skin over a girl's wrist.

These days her face changes like the moon,
a glowing distance, a coming and withdrawing.
I fold clothes, and she perches at the edge of the bed
growing her own skin, tossing off the small
vestiges of me like a primordial tail.
When she was born, the colours shifted in her eyes:
dust to earth, as if she were becoming more solid
within my gaze. How carelessly I held her,
like the earth shouldering the skies.
Suddenly I realize

all the thousands of ways I will lose
her, and I am overcome, as by a death,
with her still sitting there, singing quietly
to her stuffed monkey. The world is astonishing
in this small room. The miracle of her child's voice,
the bounty of clean clothes. All there is to give, to take.
I am staggered by the hours that disappear like small coins.
I am a spendthrift with holes in my pockets, and I know that
I have swallowed too much happiness, it is an ache,
that if I stepped out of my body I would break

into blossoms. And so why not? The garden
blooms until frost has bitten off the last petals,
stubbornly, and without purpose.
Here, we are that same obtuse profusion
of colour and excess. My daughter comes to me
and I would like to fold her in my arms, show her the awesome
strength of my love. But she is skittish with my affection.
Children are wild things, lightly tamed. All I can offer
her is myself, about to soften
into blossom.

Katherine Bitney A cold snowy Sunday. A day for art and contemplation. Thinking about the conjunctions of water and air. Snow, for instance. Water locked in cold air

Like · Comment · Share · Yesterday at 8:46am

Snow falls
like ashes:

the lost body
of water.

It can only find itself
on our tongues.

Rosalie has poked you.

Poke Back

I visit just after the aneurysm,
when words are moths
that flutter around your shaved
skull, whispery wings
that could mean moon,
or night, or death. How to choose?

When your daughter called me,
she was too grief-stricken for panic;
every muscle in her body
sore from holding hope
at an arm's length, a brimming
glass she couldn't spill or set down.

Now you,
with the same delicate and agonizing
control, catching and releasing
the small, dusty-winged creatures
of language,

and our cups overflow.

Dave Hickey wonders if his tv misses him.

Look: my heart is a moving picture of murders
and Nutella. Your heart a mute witness.

Look: there is enough light within me
to fill a room. Outside, people stare
through the window at our reflection,
a tattoo of blue needling your face.

Look: my stories unwind like ticker tape
thrown from a building. There is too much
to catch. You stand below and watch
a confetti of lives fall at your feet.

Look: A child, with a belly-full of air, flies;
A swifter Swiffer; Two and a Half Men;
dismembered, a woman screams in a language
that can mean only grief, or terror.

Look: the sun will kill you. So will
fish, plastics, and cell phones. I will tell you
the cause of SIDS at five o'clock. Don't
put your baby down before that.

Look: even when you leave, even when
my face is a starless night, look.

Marita Dachsel Whoa. Just heard a gunshot
outside!

Like · Comment · Share · 11 hours ago

In the small wood shelter, listening
for the school bus, we'd hear the soft crack
of a rifle, like a baseball hitting the sweet spot.
Somewhere close, a deer
falling into leaves.

Now the same crack, without the brush
and grass to tender it. Blocks away
someone is falling

minutes after I put my boy to bed.
This day of backyard leaves,
wasps getting drunk from apples
rotted on the sidewalk,

someone is falling, tender knees on
concrete, wild carrot springing
from the cracks. Remember the heart-skip,
waiting for the bus, hearing

the fall, even though you couldn't have
possibly. On the bus you forget
any sound but the droning of the wheels
against gravel. Lean your head against
the cold metal of the window

in your bedroom. The cars hum distant
as stars. You forget.

Rob McLennan is trying to put everything back
together;

The house reveals dark patches
of memory, paint that isn't worn
by the sun's constant gaze.
Your father is stuck here,
in a house with all its loss
exposed.

Your mother's things packed away, and no matter how
you rearrange it: absence
cut clear, like the outline of dust
around her missing jewelry box:
a fingerprint in reverse.

And now you are in your own home.
Your father's breath echoes
into the phone. He talks about
the lawn's growth, and how the neighbour's
casserole wasn't bad.

You are bent over your daughter's puzzle,
a thin piece of cardboard sticking
to your palm as your father's
voice unravels. Her small hands
turn the pieces without hesitation,
slips each jigsawed part into a neat
rectangle, a retaining wall.

She is like her grandmother,
turning dough with muscled hands,

competent and easy. The casual way
she folded flour and yeast into
the miracle of bread rising
alone in its own patch of sun.

You are still holding the last piece
when she takes it from you,
fits it into the far edge. The picture is perfect,
a gingerbread house, marshmallow smoke.
Your father's voice is already
a practiced steady.

She waits a minute, then sweeps the whole thing
off the table, watches it crumble
in mid-air.

George Murray Adventures in Bar Writing, #9984: The Guy at the Next Table Rummaging Through His Bag Who Produces, In Order, a Copy of Anna Karenina, a Pad of Paper, a Box of Condoms, and a Box of Imodium.

Like · Comment · Share · 38 minutes ago

He's a magician of the ordinary,
slowly unveiling his life,
Imodium for doves. Small flourishes
of nonchalance.

It reminds me of my mother:
the industrial sized box of tampons,
alone and defiant, inching its way
along the conveyor belt.

Twelve years old, and I was a sommelier
of shame. Every delicate note
of ignominy balanced on my tongue,
a long, bitter finish.

His condoms leer at me.
I avert my eyes, retreat to
the virtuous salt and pepper, the modest beer.

He reaches into his bag again,
and everyone in the bar watches
as he turns out another threadbare
pocket of his life.

He's that kid, the one who gets
an erection during math,

the one who wears track pants
and doesn't have the sense to hold
a binder with him at all times.

The kid we called a masturbator,
the one we tortured in slow,
sure movements.
The one who deserved it,
for exposing us all.

Brian Bartlett "Earth was found to be responsible for the asymmetric bulge of the moon's Lunar Farside Highlands. Sleep-deprived honeybees waggle-dance less accurately. A flutist stole 299 rare bird skins from a museum to pay for a new flute. The U.N. announced plans to launch a satellite powered by feces. Satsuma snails with counterclockwise shells are less likely than clockwise-shelled snails to be eaten by snail-eater snakes."

Like · Comment · Share · 8 hours ago

The moon pulls towards you,
grows a bulging heart on its sleeve,
or perhaps a cancer.

It circles the earth, and from behind thick clouds
shamefacedly watches
the tide undress the sand;

oh, even the bees are drunk
tonight, rotted apples
in a grass still;

they are so tired
of each other, of trying
to dance their way into

saying something more than:
here. I found it here. The bees
wonder if they will ever be found.

Birds molt right out of their skin,
before they realize they cannot grow another.
Still the pied piper tries to play

them new bodies of music. The town
believes in him, believes we can make
rats into children, feces into

fuel. It can happen: the moon
shudders, the bees drop in mid-
flight. Skinned birds sing

and the snail circles himself,
clockwise, tight as a fist,
until he is

the drumbeat
inside another's
coiled body.

Carolyn Smart thinking of Bronwen Wallace and the 21 years gone by.

Like · Comment · Share · on Tuesday

that harder wisdom
you are rediscovering now
some people are a country
and their death displaces you.
                    Bronwen Wallace's "Coming Through"

Last walk of the evening, and the dog lags in long, slow steps.
This summer has set the stars to panting.
The leash is loose, and the dog is having a desultory affair
with the post. We are both in love.
My steps recite your words and the sidewalk glimmers with your genius.
The dog and I imagine love in lost messages. What have we become?
I place you in each of the lighted windows,
washing dishes, talking on the phone, the cord twisting.
You are in none. It is fearsome,
that harder wisdom.

Let me start again.
In China girls could be married to
a ghost-husband.
An empty house, a wandering spirit, a girl.
She recites the language of marriage
and so it becomes one. Every night she imagines him touching her brow.
Somehow our lives are transformed
when we are just pretending to live them.
There is only one way to love but there is no how.
You are rediscovering now

the lessons in grieving what was never
yours. Our hearts are worn pockets,
the kind children fill with pebbles and feathers
because they have nothing of their own.
So it is with love.
If not pebbles, let's say, comfrey.
Your words can still knit the bones,
but the ache of you is a ghost in the marrow.
You once said, and now I see,
some people are a country

and their deaths displace you.
This is true even for places
we have never known. Our aches are named as cliffs,
and fields full of Marram grass. Your death was a tectonic shift;
we had to redraw all the maps.
All I have of you are history books, glossy brochures I knew
by heart. Lessons you have taught me by example:
there are some people
you could have trusted your life to,
and their death displaces you.

Lynn Crosbie The man on my street with a 9 month JR/ Is rough around the edges but smiles like a star.

Like · Comment · Share · a few seconds ago

Every window on this street is a diorama:
cut-out figures flicker
with our own movements.

You know nothing
about the people who surround you
except their morning faces,
brittle by the mailbox
as they leave their cardboard homes.

How can they be the same as
the woman's screened voice,
words sticky and heavy as August air.
He's going to leave her.
You can tell by the way
she drags her sighs out
like a body, cold evidence.
You can't hear his end
of the conversation, but you imagine
his voice, florescent lights to the autopsy

like that other one, last Saturday,
the stutter of her head against (a closet?
dry wall?) and someone calling the cops
before you. You, sitting up, trying to decide
how bad it has to get before you reach
for the phone. The thin layer of shame
that curtains your windows as even now
your lids pull back the dream you were working on

like the kid down the street, nine months?
ten? The man you couldn't look in the eye,
tattoos, a scar across his left cheek,
pushing the stroller, his son heavy-headed
and perfect, sleeping through all his afternoon walks.

Sue Fisher My sister, Eleanor, has been visualizing killer laser beams which she uses to attack the cancerous mass in her abdomen. Tomorrow morning, a surgeon will, in a much more conventional manner, remove it — along with a goodly portion of her innards. I don't know if visualization works, but would you please join me between 8 & 9 am Eastern with your own mental phasers set to kill? Thanks. Die cancer, die.

Like · Comment · Share · Yesterday at 7:13pm

For the first operation
I imagined the doctor as a thief,
the kind you see in heist movies;
darkly handsome, light-fingered.
Tipping rhinestones out of the box
in a glittering shower
and prying up the velvet-lined false bottom.

By the third, I knew the truth:
all they could do was smash through a window,
grab everything in sight. There is no
gloved hand, no stethoscope on the
whirring lock.

After the operations, the doctors
would tell us in hushed voices
that they thought they got it all
and we would be ushered in
to see you, your eyes glassy
with morphine, your breath
small clouds in a clear mask.

So this is all there is:
glass shards scattered over the floor,
your dressers overturned, the morning spent
naming what you have lost,
the missing T.V. and your camera with all the pictures
of your daughter's birthday party.

What is left? Only the knowledge that a stranger
has touched your nightgown, someone has taken
your mother's gold ring. The certainty
that you've been robbed.

Ian LeTourneau just filled out the census.

Like · Comment · Share · 13 hours ago

1. How many persons usually live at this address? List their ages.

My wife, though she is behind a closed door. Behind the door she is weaving, or spinning, or stitching together stuffed birds. When she comes to bed her fingers bleed and small tufts of crane feathers follow her. A chill blows through the old wood frame, a slow seep. When the snow drifts pile against it, ice crystals bloom on the window. This is beginning to happen all year long, so I can't say if she's aged or not.

My daughter, though she also lives elsewhere. Every evening her shoes are worn through, and her clothes snag on air. I've seen her in a parking lot, a hundred years old and stick-thin. Weary. She drinks coffee and I find her hair in the sink, brittle and translucent. And sometimes she's five, but only at night, when I stand by her door and watch the soft cage of her chest rise and fall. A grate around the whispering embers of her heart, a banked fire.

There is a ghost, too. He is a creature of habit, he can't shake the idea that he should be living. But he can only remember how to be born and how to die. A thousand births and deaths every morning, but he's forgotten the in-between bit. The grass and baseball and love and even a good steak sandwich. And so he's very, very old, and too young to count.

Michael Leary wonders whether facebook attracts the most spirited, happy and truly blessed or that they are made so by virtue of simply being on facebook. How do you squeeze in so many parties, so many concerts, art openings, barbeques, picnics, and so much love and so many pictures? I'm exhausted just reading about it.

Like · Comment · Share · 14 hours ago

We bare our smiles at the
barbecue. Smiles that have clearly travelled
in cars without air conditioning.
Our grins stutter as we run
out of gas, and cartoon
smoke pours from our ears.

Behind us the children pluck
wings from a fly. The fly is left behind,
spinning thickly like a drunk
winding up to hit someone.

In the long beach grass, the kids
find a used condom, purple.
They poke it with a stick, like we used
to do to dead fish, one milky
eye gazing at us, benevolent.

Someone is crying, quietly.
An adult's simpering wheeze
like a mosquito at the ear. It is my
sister, or her husband, or
their quiet marriage
which has developed a fondness

for cutting, an addiction of scars.

Unfold the picnic basket,
and set out the watermelon.
The adults are planning murder-suicide
and the children are drowning in the lake.

Index

Acknowledgements:

I'm grateful to the Ontario Arts council for its support during the writing of these poems. Many of these poems have also found a home in *CV2, Vallum Magazine, The Antigonish Review, Prairie Fire, A Crystal Through Which Love Passes: Glosas for P.K. Page*, and Friend. Follow. Text. Thank you to the editors of these publications.

Thanks as well to my professors and peers at UBC, especially Susan Musgrave, whose insights have made me a better writer. Thank you to Andrew Gray, who always finds a way to come through. Many thanks to Stuart Ross (Queen's Writer in Residence), whose editorial input was invaluable. Thanks as well to Ron Smith, for his keen eye and talent, and for letting me blame all my typos on my cat. My gratitude to Randal Macnair, for cheerily putting up with me yet again.

No one writes by themselves, so thank you to the community of writers who have supported me with such humour, love, and fantastically spot-on critiques. The Villanelles: Kirsteen, Jane, Heather, Sadiqa, Wayne, Susan, and Ashley. And of course, Sheri Benning, my first mentor and best buddy. Thanks too, to my neighbours John, Harriet, Matt, and Kendra for the sustaining food and gallons of wine.

Thanks, hugs, and smooches to my husband/editor Tim, and to my daughter Abby, both of whom are all sorts of wonderful.

This project also owes a debt of gratitude to the friends and strangers alike whose status updates have provided inspiration for these poems.

Sarah Yi-Mei Tsiang is the author of *Sweet Devilry* (Oolichan Books), which won the Gerald Lampert Award for best first book of poetry in Canada and was nominated for the Re-Lit award. Her work has been published widely in journals and anthologies, and appears in *Best Canadian Poetry 2013* (Tightrope books). She is the editor of the all-Susan anthology *Desperately Seeking Susans*, as well as the forthcoming anthology *Tag: Canadian Poets at Play* (Oolichan Books). Sarah is also a children's author and essayist. Her new Young Adult novel, *Breathing Fire* (Orca Books), is forthcoming in Spring 2014.